Make *Believe*

A Book of Costume and Fantasy

Costume Design
Bill Doggett

Photography
Thomas Heinser
Peter Fox

Jock McDonald
Marco Nicoletti
Ed Young

Klutz Press / Palo Alto, California

Design and Art Direction:
MaryEllen Podgorski
Illustration:
Sara Boore, Lucy Sargeant,
Elizabeth Buchanan, Ed Taber
Graphic Production:
Elizabeth Buchanan, Nakamura Graphics,
Jan Seals, Eileen Stolee
Sourcing and Manufacturing:
DeWitt Durham

Book manufactured in Singapore.
Box and contents, China and Taiwan.

Write Us.

Klutz Press is an independent publisher
located in Palo Alto, California and
staffed entirely by real human beings.
We would love to hear your comments
regarding this or any of our books.
(We have many. If you would like a
catalogue, just drop us a note.)

Klutz Press
2121 Staunton Court
Palo Alto, CA 94306

ISBN 1-878257-65-X
(The Fancy Box)
ISBN 1-877882577-68-4
(The Adventure Box)
4 1 5 8 5 7 0 8 8 8

Contents

ntroduction

It's an average morning: You wake up and find the bedroom floor has been turned into boiling red-hot lava. While you're dealing with that, you hear a familiar voice, hollering from downstairs. It's your stage manager, telling you the curtain's going up in five minutes. At breakfast, an urgent call from the castle: The annual ball has been scheduled for tonight. Everyone's dying to know, what will you be wearing? A little later, you go out on the lawn and kick a soccer ball. Instantly, a pro scout comes running toward you waving a contract and a big checkbook.

If these are your kinds of problems, this is your kind of book. In it, you will find solutions to the familiar situations you have to deal with every day: A forest fire has erupted in your back yard and you'll be parachuting into it. What to wear? Clutching flowers, a pack of pathetic princes are at the front door, moaning and crying your name. Should you bother with any of them? A naval battle has broken out in the tub. Is it better to go down the drain, or swim for the soap dish and return to fight another day?

Handling these kinds of varied situations takes the right kind of clothing and equipment. As it happens, you have everything you need right there in the house—or nearly everything. Instructions for putting it all together are quite simple (minutes in most cases) and are in the pages that follow. For those key items that you don't have right at hand, we have two magic words of advice:

Thrift Stores

We believe in thrift stores. A lot of what was photographed in this book was found in them. Our sincere recommendation to you is to find a good one and don't forget where it is. Stop in from time to time and keep an open mind, looking for the possibilities: A grandmother's set of lace curtains makes a fine wedding train. An old choir robe looks great on a wizard.

Here's a shopping list we used in our store. Obviously it's only a start, and you should customize it to your own needs, but it might help you get in the right frame of thrift store mind.

▲ Hats of every kind ✏ Ties (good for everything from ninja headbands to bird feathers) ✳ Lace curtains or tablecloths ✪ Beads, brooches, cameos, medals, etc. ◆ Funny shoes ✿ Feathers, veils ⚘ Weird wigs ♥ Scarves and shawls of all kinds ● Big belts, pouches, evening bags ★ Robes ☛ Dress shirts ✾ Frilly blouses, skirts ✱ Loud jackets, pants, shorts, shirts ♣ Too-big black pants and sport coats

Your house is full of costumes and props. Prowl around, check with the grown-ups and then use a little imagination. The only rule: Don't look at anything the way you're supposed to. Look for what it can be, not what it is.

A Giant Wind-Up Key
(cardboard and foil)

Sponge Bow Tie

Grocery Bag
Hats

Goggle Bug Eyes

Button Jewelry
and Bottle
Bracelets

Shoebox Shoe

Super*heroes*
and *Sports* Stars

Wonder Girl

Start with a leotard and tights. Add a big belt or two. Pin a large square of fabric to the back of the shoulders, and cut a headband out of construction paper. *Shazam*.

Tape ends together.

8

Scarlet Avenger

Cut a garbage bag into a square and pin in place for a cape.

The mask comes from a scrap of felt. The headband comes from Dad's old tie collection. The black cape comes from a box of big plastic garbage bags and the style comes with the territory.

Use tape to put your super letter on your shirt.

TARZAN & SHEENA

Towels of the Jungle: Two towels pinned together at the shoulder and wrapped with a cord at the waist. We splotched leopard spots on ours with black tape.

The T-shirt System: Start with a huge T-shirt. Stick your head *and* arm through the headhole. Our T-shirt was an old one, so we could paint it up with tempera paints, but you may not be so lucky.

Fabric Square Approach: A square of fabric the size of a big towel, a cord for the belt, a few safety pins, and you're all set. Paint your fabric if you can.

Scrunch a corner and pin it to your T-shirt. Rest of fabric wraps around behind.

NINJAS

An old white dress shirt from Dad's closet gives you the basic look, but it helps to tie a few strips of fabric around the arms and waist. The mask is cut from felt (see page 9). After that, just hit the streets.

ZAP!

KA-POW!

Equestrienne

We used a white shirt, a homemade ribbon tie and a biggish pair of tan pants we had to gather in the back with a safety pin.

We made a riding crop with black tape on a cardboard tube (the kind that comes off those cheap coat hangers). Boots are nice if you have them, and we dressed up a baseball helmet with a bit of ribbon.

Tally ho.

CHEERLEADER

Use strips of paper for the pompoms. Tape the bottoms together for handles. Colored tape can be used to make a sweater letter.

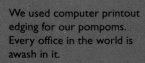

We used computer printout edging for our pompoms. Every office in the world is awash in it.

Rock Climber

The hardware sling is the key ingredient here; everything else is just style. We used nylon webbing, but a big leather belt will do as well. Throw it over one shoulder and clip on all sorts of clanking hardware kinds of stuff. We emptied a kitchen junk drawer.

SPEED DEMON

For the windblown look, stiffen a scarf with a piece of coat hanger wire. Then strap on some goggles and floor it.

Tape the wire to the wheelchair and safety pin it to the scarf.

The flames are just cardboard we cut up and painted.

Power Hitters

The baseball shirt is a pajama top worn with grey or white sweatpants. Stuff the pants into some grown-up's hiking socks, add a cap, and grab your bat and glove.

MUSCLE Dude

Rather than pumping all that iron to get the real ones, make insta-muscles out of balloons, or a cut-in-half tennis or sponge ball.

The moustache is cut from a shoebox.

For some easy-to-lift dumbbells, tape balloons to cardboard tubes from coat hangers.

18

THE CHAMP

Gym trunks, high tops and a bathrobe. The shiner is face paint, but you could use eyeliner pencil. Paper towels or old white socks wrapped around the hands are, of course, very important.

Hockey Player

The most critical ingredients here are: bike helmet, broom or hockey stick and oven mitts. The pinned-on-knee hot pads are nice, but not essential. You can make a puck out of jar lids and black tape.

BASKETBALL SUPERSTAR

All you need is a BIG tank top (we used a woman's tank dress) plus a grown-up with a strong back and a weak mind. Climb on his shoulders, pull down the tank top, and go for the slam.

Ballerinas,
Brides *and*
Fancy Ladies

Jazz dancer

You'll need: a leotard, safety pins and two scarves or pieces of fabric.

Pin the top edges of both pieces of fabric to the right shoulder of your leotard. Drape one piece across the front and pin it at the left waist. Pin the bottom corners of the second piece in a loop around your right wrist.

Newsprint Ballerina

This one takes a bit of time, but newsprint has never looked so elegant.

You'll need: plenty of newspaper, a stapler, tape, scissors and safety pins.

Start with three sheets of newspaper, folded in half to make six layers. Cut the open edge in zigzag points.

Fold the newspaper into 3" fan folds.

Fold tape over.

Staple on the tape.

Repeat and chain together until the whole tutu is long enough for the stapled edge to go around your waist. Tape and staple the ends together. Safety pin the tutu onto your leotard to keep it from falling down.

ISLAND DANCER

For the cuffs, fold a piece of construction paper in half. Cut strips as shown. Tape around wrist or ankle.

The sarong is a flowered pillow case; open the seams as shown.

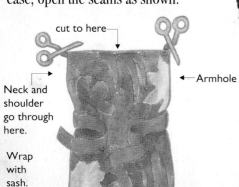

cut to here

Neck and shoulder go through here.

← Armhole

Wrap with sash.

FLAPPER

1. For the skirt, use two large squares of fabric. Fold each like this.

2. Pin the folded edge around your waist.

3. Let the extra hang loose.

4. Do the same with second piece; pin it at the other side.

Tie a scarf around your head as shown, add a really *long* necklace and plenty of rhinestone jewelry.

Le Trashbag Tutu

Put on your tights and leotard, then add this fancy tutu. All you need is a package of drawstring kitchen trash bags—we picked the pretty colored ones.

Pull the drawstring on two bags. Tie the loops of one bag around one loop of the other in a double knot.

Tie the untied bag around the loop of a third bag. Keep tying loops until you have enough skirt to go around your waist.

Cut the bottoms of the bags in an attractive zigzag or leaf shape.

Cut the ends of the loops so they make a fringe around the top of the tutu.

Use the same tying method to make a pouf headpiece out of two bags. Cut them in short zigzags and fluff them out. Bobby pin through the knot.

SAFETY NOTE: Plastic trash bags are a choking hazard for very young children.

Bubble Tutu

You'll need: a long strip of 36" wide bubble wrap, clear tape, a stapler, glue and some safety pins.

Fold the bubble wrap in half lengthwise. Fold the top layer in half again. Use a little glue or tape in spots to hold it.

Pleat the folded edge in 3-inch folds. Tape the pleats, then staple through the tape on both sides of each fold. Continue until there is enough to go around your waist.

Pin the tutu to your leotard in a few places for support.

Wand: Scrunch a small piece of bubble wrap and tie it in the middle.

Fluff it out to make a nice pouf. Tape it to a chopstick and add some ribbons.

You can make a hair ornament the same way, and bobby pin it to your hair.

Bubbly Bride

Wrap thrift store white curtains around your waist for a skirt. Wear a pretty white blouse; add gloves and pearls if you have them.

For the balloon or flower wreath, use a wire bent into a circle about an inch bigger in diameter than your head. Blow the balloons up small and tie them with as much "tail" as possible. Carefully tape them (white first-aid tape works great) to the wire in a spiral pattern. Add some bright ribbons down the back.

Blushing Bride

Because we are thrift store believers, we had a round tablecloth to use for the train. If you are not so lucky, an old sheet or bedspread will work almost as well.

1. Fold your tablecloth or sheet, (or bedspread) as shown.

2. Wrap the folded edge around your waist and pin together at the red dots.

3. Any kind of white blouse and skirt work for the dress, especially if you have something lacy to use for a shawl. For a veil, it's hard to beat a half-slip.

A Tissue Bouquet

1. Stack six layers of toilet paper each four squares long.

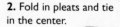

2. Fold in pleats and tie in the center.

3. Fluff the tissue, one layer at a time.

Swooning Princess

A perfect outfit for dropping hankies, spurning suitors, slaying dragons, falling into waiting arms, defying the king…etc, etc.

You'll need: one old sheet, about 12 feet of cord, and a large piece of construction paper.

I. Cut a slit in an old sheet as shown.

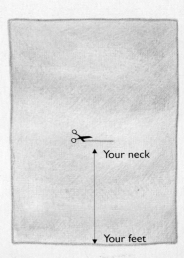

Your neck

Your feet

2. Stick your arms straight out. Get a friend to arrange the sheet on you as shown.

3. Put the middle of your cord around the back of your neck. SAFETY NOTE: If the cord is strong enough to be a choking hazard, cut it in half and safety pin the halves together so it has a place to break apart easily.

4. Wrap the cord over your shoulders, under your arms, and cross on the back of your waist …

5. …cross on the front of your waist, then in back again, and finally, tie in front.

Hat and Veil

Cut a quarter circle from a large piece of construction paper. Tape together where shown and decorate with ribbons, paint, glitter, jewels…etc.

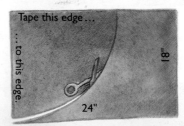

Tape this edge…

…to this edge.

18"

24"

For the all-important veil, pin a sheer scarf or piece of fabric to the top of the cone. We used elastic under the chin to keep our hat on.

Our Best Tutu

Although we list several quick tutus elsewhere in the book, there comes a time when nothing but the real thing will do. What follow are the instructions for a complete, sewn-together tutu.

You'll need: a piece of ⅝" wide elastic exactly as long as your waist, 3 yards of 60" wide net nylon* (if your waist is bigger than 25 inches, use 4 yards of net), a needle and strong thread.

A sewing machine can make things quicker if you know how to use one.

1. Overlap the elastic one inch…

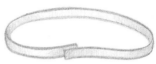

…and sew it securely to itself.

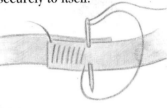

2. Cut the net into four long strips each 15 inches wide.

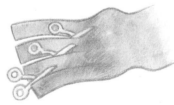

If the net is wrinkly, now is the best time to iron it.

*You could also use different colors of net for a fancier tutu.

3. Take two of the strips of net and lay one on top of the other.

Sew a loose gathering stitch with sturdy thread down the center of both layers. Repeat with a second thread, ¼" beside the first. (A sewing machine will really speed up this part.)

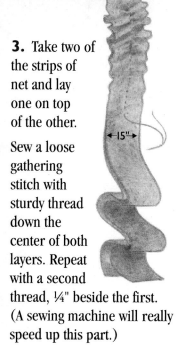

4. Pull the threads to gather the net as tightly as you can Don't break the gathering threads!

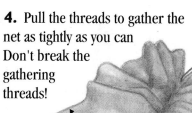

5. Stretch the elastic tightly over a board, a cardboard box or a large chair back. It needs to be pretty tight.

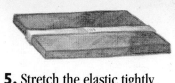

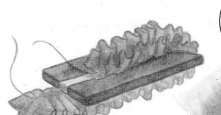

6. Adjust the length of the gathered net to match the stretched elastic.

7. Sew the net to one edge of the stretched elastic, using a lockstitch every quarter-inch.

Lockstitch

8. Repeat steps 3 through 7 with the other two pieces of net. Sew the gathered net to the other edge of the stretched elastic.

33

9. Put on your tutu and dance!

Monsters,
Meanies
and Mutations

Countess Dracula

Wear black pants and a white shirt—turn the collar up and tie a skinny black ribbon bow tie. Put on a black jacket.

Make a cape by cutting a batwing edge to a black plastic trash bag.

Brush your hair back from your face. If you are lucky enough to have some, use white face paint for that bloodless look. Add some black on brows, eyes and lips. A thin red dribble is a tasty final touch. Now go downstairs for a quick bite.

MASKED MARAUDER

A sleeve cut from an old T-shirt just needs a nose-notch and two eyeholes to make a superhero mask.

Cat Burglar

Start with the basics: dark pants, sweatshirt and watch cap. Then rub a little black face paint (or eye shadow) under your eyes. Keep to the shadows.

al Minestrone

The white tie is the real key to this look. Use a bathrobe belt if you have to. After that, add a dark shirt and a baggy jacket if you can. The violin case and Rolls are nice, but it's that cold look around the eyes that's really essential.

the 3-Leg Dude

Head Turner
The basic backwards look. Wear it down to dinner and start with dessert.

To make the third leg, turn one leg of a pair of pants inside out and stuff it inside the other one. (This sounds confusing, but it will make sense when you do it.) Stuff it a little more with some crumpled newspaper, then pin a shoe to the bottom. Belt the new leg to your side. We don't know where he got the third arm.

Handwalker

You'll need: a big hooded sweatshirt, sweat pants, a lunch bag, newspaper and lots of safety pins.

Take off your shoes. Put on a large hooded sweatshirt as if it were pants. Make sure the hood is in front, and only let your toes stick out of your sleeves.

Pin a stuffed lunch bag into the hood of the sweatshirt.

Stuff the sweat pants legs with crumpled newspapers. Pin your shoes to the cuffs. If you're lucky you'll have the stretchy kind of sweat pants you can see through. If not, you'll need to cut eyeholes in the seat, or just stumble around blindly.

You'll need help for this part. Raise your arms. Put the pants over your arms and pull them over your head. Pin the sweatshirt to the pants all around and pin the hood up so that the head looks natural. If your arms get tired use two brooms or mops instead. Hold the sticks (kind of like stilts) as you walk.

1. Cut a wire hanger like this

and bend the bottom piece to look like this:

(Fit the curve to your head.)

2. Get a second hanger, the kind that has a cardboard tube. Pull off the tube and cut it in half.

3. Stick the halves on your frame and decorate it with glue, tape, construction paper and feathers.

ARROW

HEAD

Fake Stab

Cardboard and glued-on tinfoil. Button inside your shirt.

NEANDERTHAL

Make a timeless costume out of fabric scraps or old blankets, cut with jagged edges. Cut head holes and drop over body.

Og's club is a bunch of grocery bags scrunched around a baseball bat and tied with twine. For ice age boots, put your feet into grocery bags and wrap with twine. Wear some big gloves inside out, if you have them.

For Og's hair, we had the incredible good fortune to find this pompom toilet seat cover in a thrift shop. Frankly, we doubt you'll be as lucky. But you can make an equally fine wig out of old shredded rags, or an old washcloth, or hand towel pinned together in layers and cut up on the edges.

Captain Blackpatch

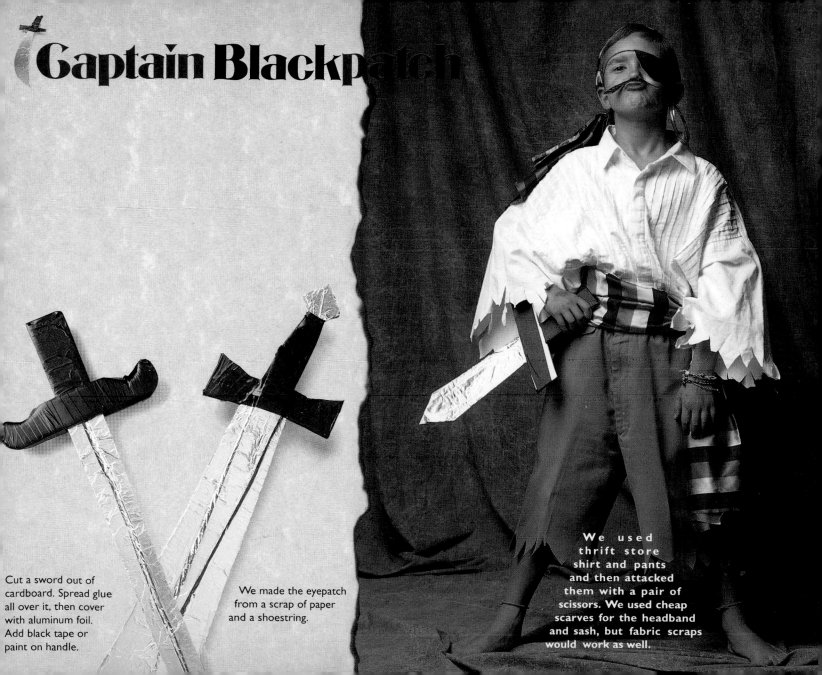

Cut a sword out of cardboard. Spread glue all over it, then cover with aluminum foil. Add black tape or paint on handle.

We made the eyepatch from a scrap of paper and a shoestring.

We used thrift store shirt and pants and then attacked them with a pair of scissors. We used cheap scarves for the headband and sash, but fabric scraps would work as well.

the One-person Piggy Back

A great costume for staggering around the house, hitting your head and scaring the dog. You probably ought to be eight or more for this one. *You'll need:* spare pair of pants, baggy shorts, tennis shoes, belt, jacket, lunch bag, baseball cap and a bunch of safety pins.

Plus a little acting ability.

1. Pull the shorts on, but not all the way, just to your knees. Pin them in place and leave the zipper open so you don't trip. The cuffs should hit the ground. Now put on a BIG sweatshirt and pull it all the way down to your waist.

Bermudas pinned to legs

2. With crumpled newspaper, stuff the sleeves of the sweatshirt and legs of the spare pants. Then belt the pants on as shown. Pin your spare tennis shoes to the cuffs of your pants (otherwise known as your fake legs.)

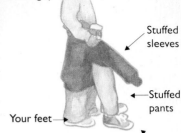

Stuffed sleeves

Your feet

Stuffed pants

Fake feet

3. Now pull the shoes up as shown and pin them in place. Then put the stuffed sleeves of your sweatshirt into place as shown and pin.

4. For the fake head, stuff your lunch bag with newspaper, pin it in place, and pin the baseball cap on it. Put the jacket on and pull it down so it hides your weird waist.

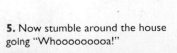

5. Now stumble around the house going "Whooooooooa!"

Little*Big*Hat

A truly great costume, but don't plan on moving around much when you're in it. The hardest part is getting the big sheet of stiff cardboard. We used a 3 foot by 5 foot piece from an art supply store.

1. Make the big hat using the instructions on page 54. Remember, it's got to go around your whole body, so think BIG. We made our hat so tall that, when he was in it, Adam had to hold it up with his outstretched arms. But you can make yours shorter so it rests on top of your head. The important thing is that it doesn't cover your stomach.

2. After that, all you need is to button a big shirt and jacket around your waist, and use face paints to paint a face on your tummy.

Headless Wonder

As you would expect, taking your head off and tucking it under one arm takes a bit of time, but there's no question it's worth every minute. The final effect will just about take your breath away. Try this suggestion: Start working on this outfit about an hour before Dad and Mom are due home, then plant yourself on the couch. Just imagine their surprise and delight when they walk through the door!

You'll need: an assistant (for sure); a *long* skirt and a button-up jacket if you're a girl; if you're a boy, a trench or overcoat plus a long pair of pants or sweats. Everyone needs a way-too-big button-up shirt, a red towel, some safety pins, plus good tape and scissors. The biggest ingredient is this: A cardboard tube that goes over your head and becomes your new shoulders. We've made them out of corrugated cardboard and posterboard. You need a piece about 48 inches wide and 24 inches tall. *Warning:* It's hard to fake this with thin posterboard or soft cardboard. Use stout materials here.

24"

48"

1. If you're using corrugated cardboard, make sure the ribs run up the 24-inch side. (It doesn't have to be a new piece—you can flatten an old carton—previous folds don't matter.) Make your cardboard flexible by rolling it into a very tight roll.

2. Roll your cardboard into a big tube (use plenty of tape). Put it on, mark where to cut for the head and shoulders, then take it off and do the cutting. Go back and forth a few times. Be picky.

Cut to fit shoulders

At least 3 inches

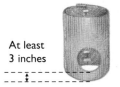

3. Cover the top of the tube with the red towel and pin or tape it in place.

4. Have your assistant place the tube on you. *Make sure it fits and doesn't slump over to one side.* Poke your head *all the way* through the hole and smile. This is the key. Make a solid-fitting tube!

5. Next, put on the too-big shirt. Pull it *over* the tube and tuck it into your pants or skirt (I told you it had to be big) and stick your head through the unbuttoned front. Your assistant should button the shirt above and below your head. Now stick just your hands— not your arms— through the shirt front. Cross your hands under your chin, thumbs out. Don't let any of your arm show.

6. Then get into your too-long pants or skirt. Pull the waist up way high— to your armpits.

7. *For the girls:* Put the jacket on over the shirt. Stuff the sleeves with crumpled newspaper and safety pin them under your chin so it looks like your hands are coming out of the sleeves.*

For the boys: The trench coat goes on now. Stuff the sleeves with crumpled newspaper and pin them into place so it looks like your hands are coming out of them and tenderly holding your head.*

8. *Everybody's last step:* Your assistant makes the final adjustments, arranging everything so it looks just so. If you've made a good solid tube, you can walk all over the neighborhood with this costume.

*You can pin gloves in the sleeves if you want to leave your hands free.

Story**book**

People

Cinderella's Carriage

We made our carriage out of foam-core board from an art supply store. A big piece of regular cardboard works too.

You'll need: two big pieces of foam-core board, (or cardboard 32" by 40"), some orange and green paints and tape.

Look at the drawings below and use a marker to freehand them onto both pieces of your board, then cut and paint away. Use tape freely to attach it to your wheelchair.

Not for use after midnight!

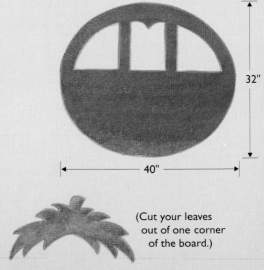

32"

40"

(Cut your leaves out of one corner of the board.)

inderella

If you're lucky, this is a costume already hiding in Mom's closet, or maybe an attic trunk. For our part, we found it in our faithful thrift store.

You'll need: a frilly blouse, a full skirt, a fluffy half-slip, 1½ yards of ribbon, a piece of cardboard, some bold paint and hopefully a pair of Cinderella-looking shoes.

Cut your crown out of cardboard (see drawing) paint it gold, staple the ends together and, if you can, glue a nice stone to the front. Get your attendants to help you into your blouse, slip and skirt, then cross your ribbon in front as shown.

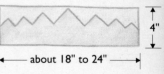

4"

|← about 18" to 24" →|

Incidentally, on page 58 you'll find some different crowns if you'd like some choices.

Captain Hook

The only *really* essential part to this costume is the hook. Everything else is nice, but optional if the Captain is in a hurry. *Tick Tock.*

The Hook:

1. Use a coat hanger and bend the wire into the shape shown here with a pair of pliers (grown-up assistant helpful).

2. Wrap with a bunch of aluminum foil. You might use glue to keep it from unwrapping.

3. Find a plastic or paper cup you can punch and cut as shown. Then cover with aluminum foil (again, glue if necessary), stick it through the cup and tape it all together.

Everything Else:

We had a thrift store bathrobe that looked nice, particularly with a frilly woman's blouse underneath. The hat you can make with directions on page 54.

Robin Hood

We used a square of green fabric for Robin's tunic, but if you have a towel you can cut up, or even a pillow case, either will do. The important thing is green. It's hard to imagine Robin wearing anything else.

You'll need: Two yards of green fabric, any kind of woodsy belt, a piece of green construction paper (12" x 18"), glue or tape and a feather.

Tunic: Fold your fabric as shown and cut a head-hole. Length should be about mid-thigh. Belt it at the waist. (A pillow case won't need folding, but it will need head and arm-holes.)

Leggings: These are optional, of course, but a nice touch. We just wrapped green strips around Robin's lower pants legs.

Hat: Cut the construction paper and fold up the edges as shown.

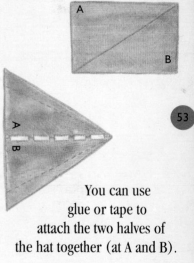

You can use glue or tape to attach the two halves of the hat together (at A and B).

53

We used elastic to keep it on. Don't forget the feather.

500 Hats

You can make a million different kinds of ■'s *by learning how to make the basic circle hat.*

Roll up front and back of brim for a Napoleonic bicorn.

For a witch hat, make a cone instead of a cylinder for the top.

The Musketeer Hat: Roll up one brim and attach a white handkerchief.

You'll need: posterboard or other sturdy paper, tape and glue, a stapler, scissors, tracing paper and a pencil.

1. Trace an LP record on posterboard and cut it out. Put a pencil mark in the center. For big hats, cut a circle a few inches bigger than an LP.

2. Measure your head.

3. You'll get a number. Match it to one of these. That gives you your head-size oval. Trace that oval onto tracing paper, and then onto your big circle of cardboard, being sure to match up centers.

19" 20" 21" 22"

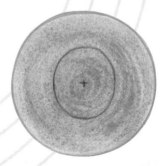

4. Cut out your oval carefully and save both the oval piece and the big circle with the oval hole in it.

For a picture hat, don't add a top at all!

5. Cut a strip of posterboard as tall as you want your hat to be, and one inch longer than your head measurement.

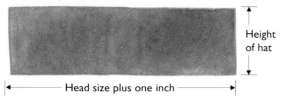

Height of hat

Head size plus one inch

6. Coil this strip until it will fit in the hole of your hat brim. Put it halfway in and adjust it until it fits snugly all around. Staple the overlap about every inch, getting close to the top and bottom.

Be sure to put a staple close to top and bottom edge.

Roll one side up for an Aussie hat, both sides up for a cowpoke hat!

7. Slide the brim to the bottom. Glue the edges where they join. On the inside, tape in a few places until the glue dries.

Glue here.

Tape here.

8. Glue the top to the sides; tape on the inside until the glue dries.

Glue.

Tape.

Fold up three sides for a tricorn hat.

9. When your hat is dry, decorate it with medals, ribbons, flowers, fruit, old silverware, buttons, paint, pipe cleaners, scarves, small animals, seashells, you name it! If you need an elastic to hold it on, carefully punch two small holes over where your ears will be. Stick the elastic through from the inside and knot it around toothpicks or bobby pins on the outside.

Roll back one edge and decorate with frills and flowers for an English garden hat.

55

Little Red Riding Hood

Two red towels and a handful of big safety pins are the only ingredients to this outfit. Pin the towels together as shown and then hide the pins by turning the hood inside out.

To keep in place, pin it once in front.

Then grab a basket, head to Granny's and DON'T talk to any wolves.

You can roll back a cuff around your face.

Three Towel Genie

A perfect outfit for granting wishes. Use one thin, medium-sized towel for the turban, and two larger towels for the harem pants.

Towel turban:

Wrap a towel around your head, with the ends at the front…

…twist the ends together…

…and pin. Thicker towels need more pins.

Harem pants: Take two towels or squares of fabric. Put the towels around your waist and tie the top corners together—one knot at front center, one at the back.

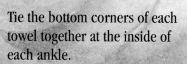

Tie the bottom corners of each towel together at the inside of each ankle.

Crystal Crown

An impressively royal crown.
Your scissors better be sharp.
A grown-up assistant is helpful.

You'll need: a two-liter plastic
soft drink bottle, a hole punch,
sharp scissors and eight or nine
paper fasteners.

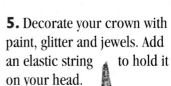

Here's a
simpler
design.

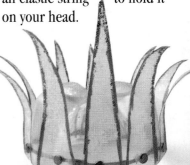

1. Remove the
label from the
bottle and cut
the top off at an
angle.

2. Cut down from the
top to the baseline to
make eight or nine
points; round the
points slightly.

3. Punch
the center of
the base of each
point with
a hole
punch.

4. Fold down
each point and punch
through its hole *through* the
base of the bottle. Put
a paper fastener
in each pair of
holes to hold it
in place.

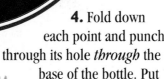

5. Decorate your crown with
paint, glitter and jewels. Add
an elastic string   to hold it
on your head.

 # SNOW WHITE

You can assemble this with stuff from your own closet or the thrift store—a puffy-sleeved white blouse, a full yellow skirt and a blue vest. Pin a red towel to your shoulders as a cape.

Avoid all

Angel

Here's the outfit for all those times when you're just being your average angelic self.

The basic robe can be a white house coat if you're in a hurry to get to heaven. But if you want to make a nicer impression when you get there, use a sheet and the instructions on page 31 for the damsel's dress.

Angel Wing Ingredients:
Two coat hangers (the kind with the cardboard tubes are the easiest); two white plastic garbage bags; tape and safety pins.

1. Cut and bend the wire hangers like so. Pinch the safety pins into place with pliers.

Hooks go over shoulders.

2. Stick the hangers into the bags, poke the hook part through the bags as shown and cut the edges in a feathery zig-zag. Keep the wings in place with tape.

3. Bend the hook part of the hangers so they can sit comfortably on your shoulders. Use the four safety pins to make them stay (you don't want your wings falling off).

Paper Plate Halo: Cut a paper plate like this:

Recycle this part.

Fit the inner circle around your head and bend the outer circle up at the back.

Emperor of the Planet

The key thing here is the right attitude—for which the hat can be a great help. The instructions for it are on page 54. Decorate it with ribbons and wear with authority.

We used bent paint brushes pinned into place for the epaulets and some cord to drape around the shoulder. For the basic foundation, we had a dark jacket and light pants, but they're really optional.

The sash is just a big square of fabric pinned into place. The medals are trinkets, earrings, ribbon and such.

61

The headband and feather are the essentials, but a beaded necklace is almost as important. We made ours by stringing radishes together since no one around here likes them. But you can use popcorn, Froot Loops,® macaroni, gummy bears...

HIGH-VOLTAGE CLOWN

A great costume for jumping out from behind a couch. You'll need a loud shirt, louder pants, ugly socks and big shoes. After that, some coffee filters and muffin cups add a nice touch.

For the collar, fold a filter in half,

then in thirds

and staple the point to a small paper plate cut like this:

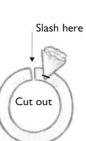

Slash here

Cut out

Repeat for the whole plate.

Button Cover: Cut this shape exactly out of a shoebox. One per button.

Button slips through here.

To decorate, we stapled cupcake cups on our button covers, but you can use your imagination.

On your head, wear a basket decorated with hair of curly red ribbon.

63

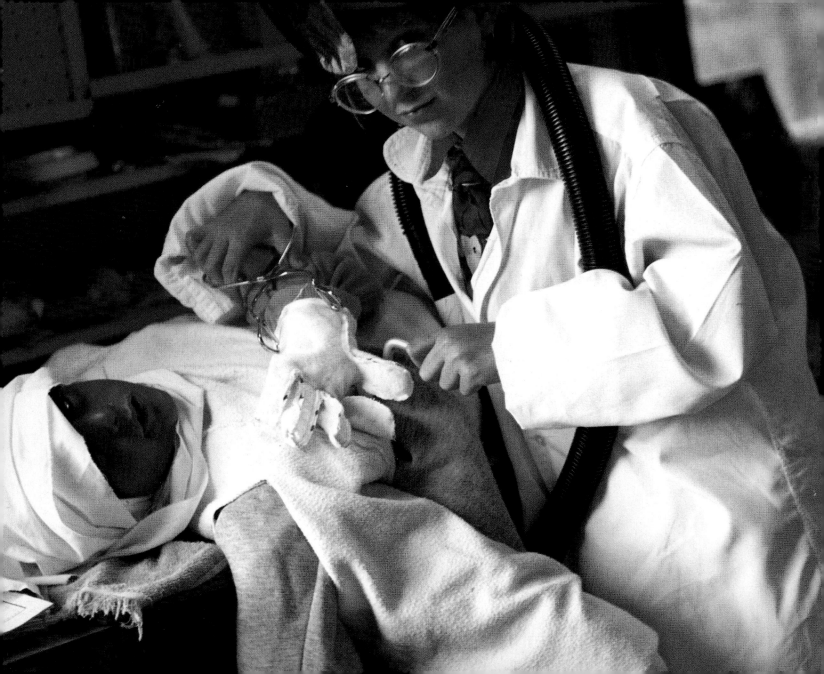

Grown-ups
and Other
Career Mistakes

POLICE OFFICER

The baton (painted paper towel tube) might be the only thing you really need for this outfit, but if you can find some kind of proper-looking hat, that should clinch it. We had a blue jacket and clip-on tie, but you might not choose to go to those lengths.

Rock Queen

DON'T
TELL
YOUR
MOTHER

Hair spray your hair up very seriously, then wrap a shawl around your shoulders, halter style. We made our microphone by poking a hole in an old tennis ball and sticking in a dead extension cord. We slipped a cardboard tube around it for a handle.

After that, it's all style.

KING

OF ROCK 'N ROLL

You'll need:

1. A big piece of stiff cardboard (we had gold!)

2. A pair of scissors and a few safety pins

3. A good agent

Draw your glasses, lightning bolt and sleeves before you try to cut. If you've only got boring cardboard, staple aluminum foil to it when you're done cutting.

Staple the sleeves together and slip them on. Pin the lightning bolt to your shirt. Tape the glasses onto your forehead (relax, it won't hurt).

Then tune up that tennis racket and turn on your amp.

ASTRONAUT

Start by dressing up in solar-reflective white (we used sweats and a thermal T-shirt, plus some high tops). Then we found a clunky belt and attached Star Trekky kinds of hardware (a garlic press and a Walkman, mostly). You will find that ski gloves will keep your hands safe from the harsh conditions of outer space.

The Helmet:
We sacrificed a plastic bucket, cut a big window in it, and then stapled it all over with aluminum foil.

Fire Fighter

If you check around, you can probably find the raincoat, boots and store-bought helmet in the house. We made the axe (and it's a very important part of the look) by drawing the outline on cardboard and cutting it out. Then we applied some paint and stapled on the aluminum foil for a keen edge.

OPERA NIGHT
Couple

For the lady, a dark housecoat that should have been thrown away long ago made a nice evening dress. The shawl is a towel. The peacock feather is a peacock feather and the shoes are Mom's cast-offs.

We started with a dark jacket and pants for the gentleman. The pants and shirt are closet fare, the jacket is Dad's. The clip-on bow tie came from the back of a drawer, although you could tie one out of an old necktie.

Cummerbund: We used a square of fabric, about a yard by a yard, and pleated it. Some masking tape held the pleats, and a safety pin secured it around the waist.

Frank 'n' Bride

Frank: Frank did the best he could for this occasion. He's wearing his favorite scarf, vest, and too-big hiking boots. The overall greenish look, plus the scars, are face paint.

Neck bolts are an absolutely key accessory. We used wire cutters to snip off the pointy ends of push pins, then stuck their plastic bases to band-aids with glue. Thread spools would do about as well.

His blushing bride: Mrs. Stein is wearing a white blouse, and for her train, a lovely set of thrift store curtains. A bouquet of dead weeds expresses the joy of the occasion. It would make a mess, and that's the reason we didn't do it, but flour in the hair makes a nice white streak.

Cowpokes

The vest is our favorite part of this outfit.
Take a grocery bag, cut it up into the appropriate
vest shape (don't forget the fringe on the bottom),
then crumple and crumple and
crumple. After five minutes of
concentrated crumpling, you'll
have a vintage old leather look.

The Sheriff's badge is cardboard,
safety pin and tinfoil.

You can make a pair of cowpoke chaps out of two towels folded down at the top corners.

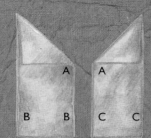

Fold and pin the points over your belt …

… then pin A to A, B to B and C to (shining) C.

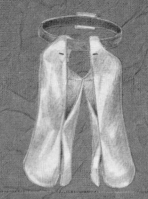

Make a belt buckle by cutting a shape out of cardboard and gluing a string design to it, then gluing aluminum foil on top.

Tape a safety pin to the back. You can make a badge the same way.

Feet, *Fruit,* Fingers *and* *Funny* Hats

Duck foot: Cut out a half circle including the clasp from a manila envelope.

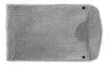

Stick your foot in the envelope and put a couple staples on either side of your ankle. Fold the red dots up behind your ankle and staple them together.

Elephant foot: Take an empty gallon milk jug. Cut off the top and part of the back. Paint the outside grey and add pink toenails.

Ms. Matched footwear: A silver evening sandal over an argyle knee sock makes a unique fashion statement.

Mummy: Wrap an old white T-shirt or rag around your leg.

Weird toes: Get four empty film cans for each foot. Stick the film can lids inside your socks and pop the film cans onto the outside for a new set of toes.

Monster feet: Use face paints and stick on some round Band-Aids for warts.

Blow-up toes: Blow up balloons, leaving some "tail," then tape the tails to your shoes. Be careful taping balloons—if the tape touches the balloon in the wrong place, it's all over when you pull the tape off!

Bunch of Grapes

Not hard—you just need lots of balloons!

You'll need: a piece of green paper, an extra-large T-shirt, safety pins, and 36 purple balloons.

Safety pin the balloons through the stem onto the T-shirt. Be careful with pins and balloons or *kabloom!*

Cut a leaf hat out of green paper.

Slash here, overlap and staple.

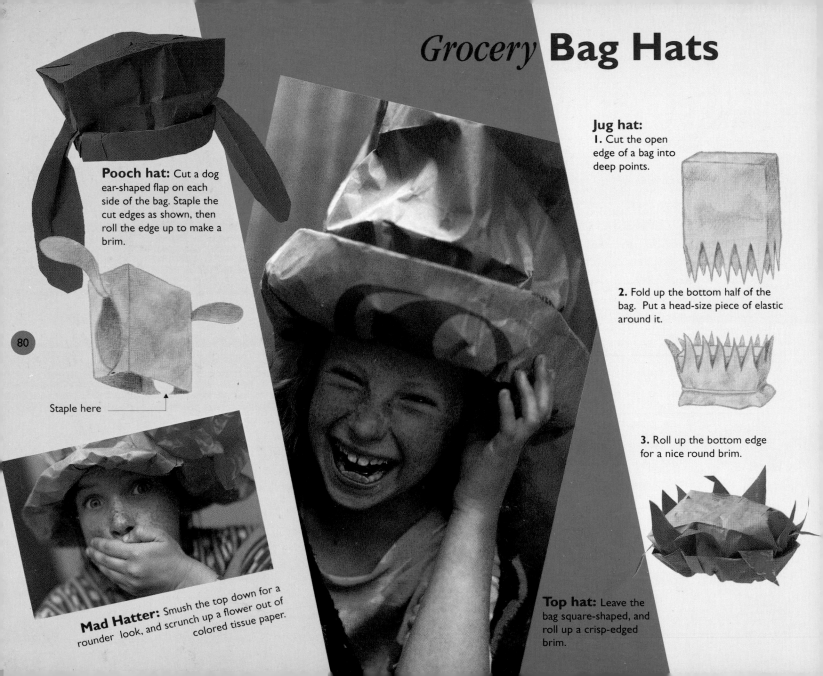

Pooch hat: Cut a dog ear-shaped flap on each side of the bag. Staple the cut edges as shown, then roll the edge up to make a brim.

Staple here

Mad Hatter: Smush the top down for a rounder look, and scrunch up a flower out of colored tissue paper.

Jug hat:

1. Cut the open edge of a bag into deep points.

2. Fold up the bottom half of the bag. Put a head-size piece of elastic around it.

3. Roll up the bottom edge for a nice round brim.

Top hat: Leave the bag square-shaped, and roll up a crisp-edged brim.

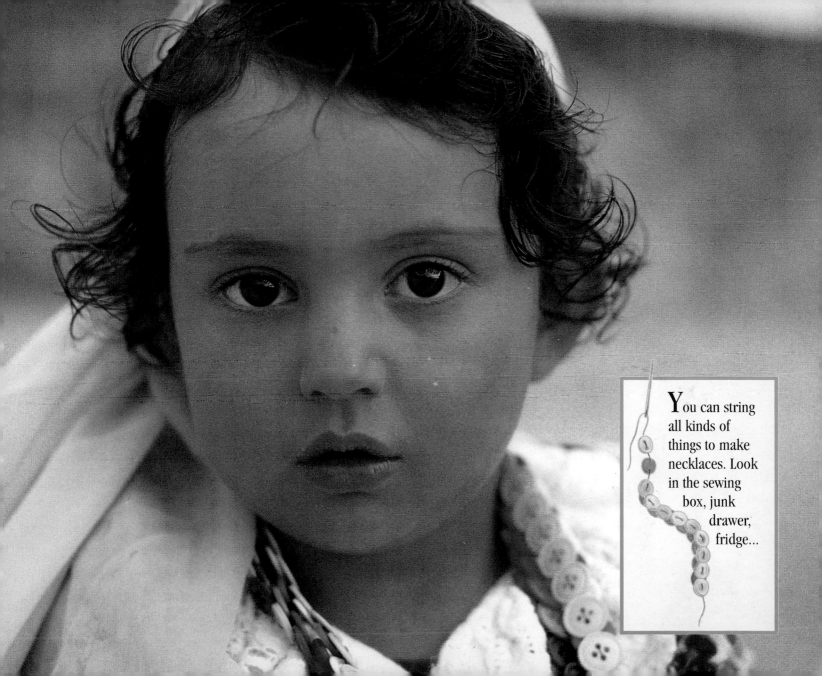

You can string all kinds of things to make necklaces. Look in the sewing box, junk drawer, fridge...

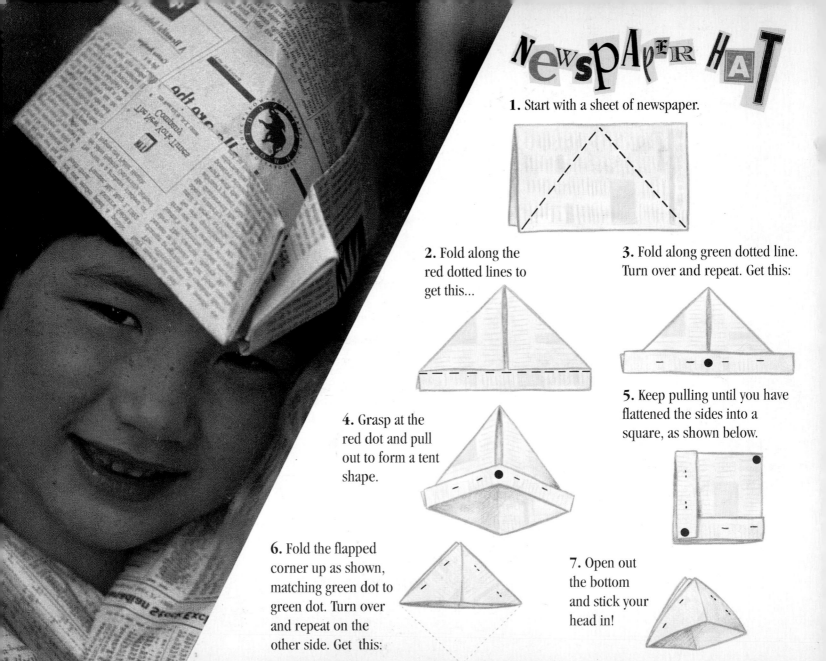

NEWSPAPER HAT

1. Start with a sheet of newspaper.

2. Fold along the red dotted lines to get this...

3. Fold along green dotted line. Turn over and repeat. Get this:

4. Grasp at the red dot and pull out to form a tent shape.

5. Keep pulling until you have flattened the sides into a square, as shown below.

6. Fold the flapped corner up as shown, matching green dot to green dot. Turn over and repeat on the other side. Get this:

7. Open out the bottom and stick your head in!

Bug antennas: Twist a wire around on the top of a headband. Or, glue straws to the headband. Use your imagination for what to put on the ends.

Chef's Hat: Staple small pleats into a white paper bag, then roll up the bottom into a small brim.

Bird Wings: For wing feathers, tie a dozen or so neckties to each arm.

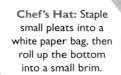

Bunny: For flop ears, attach two knee socks to a headband. Put a pair of white ankle socks over your hands for paws. Use face paint to make whiskers and a nose.

Bubble Fingers: Blow up balloons (don't tie them) and pull them over your fingertips.

The Kids' Credits

The following kids and teens lent us their happy faces to appear in our book. We'd like to thank them one and all by name: Ali Ardie, Halim Ardie, Rosie Bassett, Kaitlin Beaver, Katherine Bechtel, Arielle Bivas, Raphael Bivas, Brandy Bland, Selia Carter, Solange Carter, Cody Cassidy, Scotty Cassidy, Anna Cheever, Jacqueline Cheever, Katherine Cheever, Nicole Cheever, Jay Cho, Sean Clay, Alex Dalal, Nina Dalal, Phillip Davis, Lauren Dey, Katherine Dey, Joey Diego, Travis Doggett, Jimmy Donnelly, Michelle Donnelly, Courtney During, Allen Edwards, Adrian Fine, Livia Fine, Kayla Fox, Naomi Frank, Whitton Frank, Rubin Gaztambide, Mikey Gold, Lindsey Gravelle, Nicholas Green, Georgia Rae Herzog, Guy Hughes, Kelsey Jessup, Lucas Johnson, Nell Johnson, Arad Kedar, Leila Khosrovi, Reid Kleckner, Paul Kvam, Peter Kvam, Alison Lee, Lily Lorentzen, Thea Lorentzen, Brian Mahoney, Kadia Usmano Martin, Knengi Usmano Martin, Laura Martinez, Noora Mashruwala, Evan Matthews, Caitlin Morrow, Stephen Morrow, Dana Murphy-Chutorian, Anne McAndrew, Molly McAndrew, Ava Nagel, Justin Nolley, Bradley Pearson, Hilary Pearson, Laura Pearson, Maren Pearson, Whitney Peterson, Carl Pitlick, Hana Raftery, Adam Riff, Michael Roberts, Leah Robinson, Patrick Robinson, Sonia Rosner, Nicholas Saria, Marshall Seaman, Samantha Goldberg-Seder, Dowd Sledge, Deirdre Smith, Latanya Smith, Michael Smith, Ariel Taymor, Danya Taymor, Speedy Terrell, Danny Watson, Michael Watson, Nicky Weiss, Molly Williams, Adam Wilson, Amy Wilson, Carrie Wilson, Julie Wilson, Aya Winston, Charlie Wolfson.

The Grown-Ups' Credits

Principle costume designer: Bill Doggett. Additional costume designers: Beaver Bauer, Callie Floor and Bryna Rifkind. Barbara Johnson coordinated nearly all of the logistics and casting. Peter Fox, Thomas Heinser and Marco Nicoletti were the location photographers. Jock McDonald was the studio photographer and Ed Young was the table top photographer. Locations were provided through the courtesy of the Elizabeth F. Gamble Gardens, First Congregational Church Nursery School, Lucie Stern Community Center and the Palo Alto Childrens' Library. The following blessed people provided their homes: Wendy and Murray Dey, Kim and Kevin Raftery, Karen and Jon Easterbrook, Vega and Steve Gerber, Vera and Wayne Horiuchi, Barbara and Karl Johnson, Leslie and Doug Murphy-Chutorian, Darcy Fuller, Lea Stublarec and Curt Peterson, Jan St. Peter and Paul Pitlick, Alic Erber and Rob Steinberg, Karin Klarreich and Walter Wilson. Interference: John Cassidy. Catering: BoJo's Popcorn Snacks.